Cambridge English Readers

···

Level 4

Series editor: Philip Prowse

The University Murders

Richard MacAndrew

D1241988

CAMBRIDGE
UNIVERSITY PRESS

CAMBRIDGE UNIVERSITY PRESS
Cambridge, New York, Melbourne, Madrid, Cape Town, Singapore, São Paulo

Cambridge University Press
The Edinburgh Building, Cambridge CB2 2RU, UK

www.cambridge.org
Information on this title: www.cambridge.org/9780521536608

© Cambridge University Press 2003

First published 2003
5th printing 2006

Printed in the United Kingdom at the University Press, Cambridge

A catalogue record for this publication is available from the British Library

ISBN-13 978-0-521-53660-8 paperback
ISBN-10 0-521-53660-X paperback

ISBN-13 978-0-521-68641-9 paperback plus audio CD pack
ISBN-10 0-521-68641-5 paperback plus audio CD pack

Contents

Characters

Inspector Jenny Logan: a police officer in Edinburgh.
Sergeant Grant: an officer helping Inspector Logan.
Sergeant Graham: another officer in the Edinburgh police.
Billy Marr: a man who lives in Edinburgh.
Helen Robertson: a police doctor.
Clare Rutherford: a research student.
Katie Jardine: a research student.
Frances (Fran) Stewart: a research assistant.
Karen Ramsay: a researcher who works at the university.
Mrs Dalwhinnie: owns Fran's flat.
Dr David Balfour: a research supervisor.
Kenneth Henderson: a research supervisor.
Tam MacDonald: a journalist.

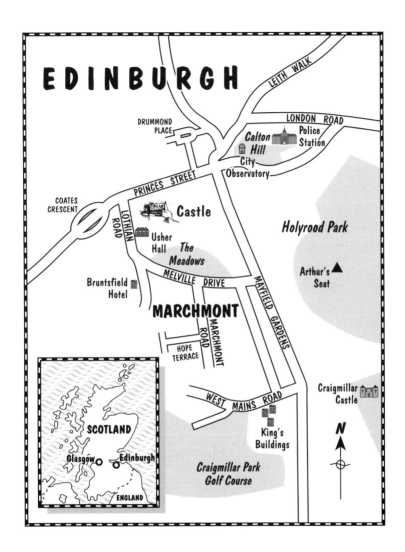

Chapter 1 *Is Billy Marr telling the truth?*

'Tell me again about this woman you killed, Billy,' said Logan.

It was late one Thursday afternoon and Inspector Jenny Logan of the Edinburgh police was sitting at her desk in the London Road police station. Opposite her was an ordinary-looking man wearing a dirty pair of jeans, a old blue pullover and a dark green jacket with holes in it. His name was Billy Marr.

'I've told you already, Inspector,' said Billy, waving a finger in the air. 'She's up on Calton Hill. I killed her with my own hands. I killed her and left her body in the grass.'

In a corner of the room by the door sat Sergeant Grant. There was a notebook on his crossed legs. But the notebook was closed and he did not have a pen in his hand. He looked bored.

'What did she look like?' he asked Marr.

Billy Marr turned to look at Grant.

'You think I'm lying, don't you? You think I'm not telling you the truth this time. Just because I've come in here sometimes when I've had a few drinks and I've told you about things I haven't really done, you think I'm making this up.' Billy turned back to Logan. 'Well, it's true this time. This time I've really done it.' He sat up straight and met Logan's eyes. 'This time I've really killed her.'

Marr's breath smelt of alcohol. Out of the corner of her

eye Logan could see Grant shaking his head slowly from side to side.

'Well, what did she look like?' asked Logan.

'She was blonde,' said Billy Marr very definitely, still looking Logan straight in the eye.

'OK,' she said. 'And how exactly did you kill her?'

'How?' repeated Marr.

'Yes, how?'

Marr looked confused for a moment. Then his face lit up. 'Like I said, with my own hands,' he said. 'I put them round her throat and I pressed and pressed.'

'You strangled her?'

'Yes,' said Marr, 'I strangled her.'

'Did you knock her out first?' asked Grant.

'What do you mean?' asked Marr.

'I mean did you knock her out? Hit her? Anything like that?' asked Grant patiently.

'No. No,' said Marr. 'Why would I do that? I just strangled her.'

Grant did not say anything. He just looked at Logan. Logan put her elbows on the desk in front of her and her head in her hands. She ran her fingers through her short brown hair and then looked up at Billy Marr. Poor Billy! He came into the London Road police station once every couple of months or so to tell the police about something he had done. Or rather had not done – because his stories were never true.

'OK, Billy,' said Logan. 'Sergeant Grant will take you downstairs and show you out.'

'Out?' said Marr. There was some surprise in his voice. 'You're not keeping me in then?'

'No, Billy,' said Logan. 'We're letting you go. You see, if you try and strangle someone and they're conscious, they fight back at you. There aren't any cuts or scratches on your face or hands where this poor blonde woman tried to fight you off. Because of that I don't think you killed anyone at all, Billy. So goodbye, and off you go!' There was an edge of anger to Logan's voice. Billy was wasting police time, but to take any action would waste even more time. The best thing to do was to listen to him and send him away.

Grant stood up and so did Marr. But then Marr pointed at Logan.

'You'll be sorry you let me go,' he said. 'I told you this time was different. This time I really did it.' And then he turned and left Logan's office with Sergeant Grant close behind him.

Logan sat back in her chair and looked out of the window. It was a cool and cloudy September day. A few leaves on the trees in the park over the road had started to change colour. Within a few weeks they would turn a rich golden brown – Edinburgh preparing for another winter. Logan hoped it would be a peaceful one but thought it unlikely – Edinburgh was a big city with all the usual problems that big cities had.

There was a quiet knock at the door and Sergeant Grant came back into the room.

'I've got rid of Billy,' he said, 'and I told him I didn't want to see him again until well after Christmas.'

Logan shook her head and smiled sadly, her anger gone.

'He's a strange one, isn't he?' she said. 'Just wanting the attention, someone to talk to. But can you actually imagine Billy killing anyone?'

Grant shook his head and started to say something but Logan's phone rang. She picked it up.

'Inspector Logan.'

Grant watched as her eyes opened wide in amazement.

'We'll be there,' she said, putting the phone down. She looked at Grant.

'They've found the body of a young woman on Calton Hill. Blonde. Dead.'

Grant's mouth opened in surprise.

'Find Billy Marr and get him back here,' ordered Logan. 'I'll get up to Calton Hill and I'll be back as soon as I can.'

Grant was already on his way along the corridor as Logan took her jacket from the back of her chair and followed him.

Chapter 2   *A discovery on Calton Hill*

The road to the top of Calton Hill goes up behind the old Royal High School, a beautiful building that in Logan's opinion should have been used to house the new Scottish government. Instead, millions of pounds had been wasted on a new building. About halfway up the hill Logan pulled her car over to the side of the road behind two police cars and an old blue Volvo. She recognised Helen Robertson, the police doctor, among a group of police officers near a wall some metres below the level of the road. As she got out of her car, Logan turned and looked up towards the Nelson Monument and the City Observatory. She thought that the view from the top of Calton Hill was one of the best over the city – well, it was when there wasn't a dead body on the side of the hill.

Walking down through the long grass by the side of the road, Logan could see the body of the young woman, lying half on her side with her back against the wall. Helen Robertson, who had been bending over the body examining it, stood up when she saw Logan arrive.

Robertson had dark hair and was wearing black trousers and a light blue blouse. She and Logan had worked together before on a number of cases and had always got on well.

'Jenny, hi!' she said. She took a deep breath. 'It's an unpleasant one, I'm afraid.'

Logan said nothing. She just looked down and studied

the body and its position. She waited for Robertson to speak.

'Young woman, blonde, mid-twenties, possibly a bit younger. I don't know who she is. She's been strangled but it wasn't done here.'

Logan looked up sharply when Robertson mentioned how the woman had died.

'The body was brought here sometime after death,' continued Robertson. 'She was also hit on the head at some time, and her hands have been tied.'

Logan bent down to have a closer look at the woman's body. She was wearing a pink T-shirt and a dark blue skirt.

'A sex attack?' asked Logan.

'I don't think so, but I can't be sure until I've done some scientific tests,' replied Helen. 'There don't seem to be any cuts or marks on the lower part of her body.'

'What about the time of death?' asked Logan.

'Again, I'll know more when I've done some tests,' said Robertson, 'but at a guess I'd say about eighteen to twenty hours ago.'

Logan looked at her watch. It was five o'clock.

'So sometime between ten and midnight last night, then.'

'That sounds right,' said Robertson. 'Look, I'll do the tests and the scientific examination first thing in the morning, and if I find anything interesting I'll give you a call.'

'Great,' said Logan, and she put her hand lightly on Robertson's arm in thanks.

Robertson bent down again and started to pack her things into a small black bag.

Logan turned and looked at the police officer standing nearest to her. She recognised him from the London Road police station but he was new and she did not know his name. He was tall with sandy-coloured hair and fair skin. Logan guessed that he was about the same age as her.

'I'm Sergeant Graham, madam,' said the officer, introducing himself. 'Davy Graham. I found the body at four twenty-five and reported it in to the station.'

'Right,' said Logan. 'Do we know who she is?'

'I'm afraid not,' said Graham. 'No bag. No wallet. No ID of any kind.'

'How did you find the body?' asked Logan

'I was on a routine call – nothing important. Anyway, as I was driving past I noticed something pink down here. It looked kind of odd. So I came over to see and it was this poor girl.'

'Who was around here at the time?'

'I don't remember anyone of any interest,' said Graham, half closing his eyes in thought. 'An old lady walking her dog. A few tourists. Nothing unusual.'

Tourists often came up Calton Hill to look at the view and to visit the Edinburgh Experience, a show about the history of Edinburgh in the old City Observatory. Even though the summer was over, there were still quite a few tourists around.

'OK,' said Logan. 'I'd like you to direct things here for the moment.'

'Right, madam,' said Graham.

'The scientists will be here soon to look round this area.' Logan pointed to the area around where the body was found. 'But I'd like you to get some more men and search the whole hill. Look for anything that might be important, but especially for a bag or wallet or ID that someone's thrown away.'

'OK, madam.'

Logan looked up towards the top of the hill.

'Has anyone been allowed to leave since you found the body?' she asked.

'Not yet, madam.'

'Good. Talk to everyone up there. Find out if anybody saw anything. Find out too if anyone was here last night between ten and midnight. I'll be at London Road. Call me when you've finished,' she said. Logan turned to take a last look at the body of the unknown girl and, as she did so, an icy feeling ran down her back. A young life had been needlessly taken away. And once again a killer was on the streets of Edinburgh.

As she walked back to her car, Logan thought about Billy Marr. Would Grant have been quick enough to catch him before he had got too far from the police station? Could he really have killed this woman? Or was it just complete chance that a body had been found on Calton Hill ten minutes after he had admitted killing someone there? As she drove back towards the police station, she wondered what Billy Marr was going to say.

Chapter 3 *Another talk with Billy Marr*

'Billy Marr is as mad as a tree full of monkeys,' said Sergeant Grant, when Logan arrived back at her office.

'You found him then,' said Logan.

'He was just round the corner – in a café on Leith Walk. When he saw me go past, he ran out after me shouting "Here I am! Here I am!"'

Logan smiled at the thought but her face quickly became serious again.

'You've had more to do with Billy Marr than me,' she said. 'Do you really think he could be a murderer?'

Sergeant Grant was sixty and had lived and worked in Edinburgh all his life. Logan had worked with him for the last four years, and she knew he had an excellent memory and was a very good detective. If there was anything useful to know about Billy Marr, Grant would know it.

'I've known Billy since he was a kid,' said Grant. 'And he's certainly an odd guy. He was strange at school and he's even stranger now. But could he kill someone . . . ?' Grant shook his head. 'I think it's very unlikely.' He looked at Logan. 'Admittedly, the dead person is a young woman and I would guess that Billy's never had normal relationships with women, but even so . . . ' Grant shook his head again. 'I'd be very surprised if it was Billy.'

Logan put her jacket over the back of her chair and moved towards the office door.

'Let's go and talk to him again,' she said. 'And we'll have

to try and forget about his regular visits here and keep an open mind.'

'Do we know who the woman is yet?' asked Grant.

'No,' replied Logan. 'We haven't found any ID.' She looked out of the window at the darkening sky. 'They're still looking up on Calton Hill but it'll soon be too dark.'

*   *   *

An hour and half later Logan and Grant were still sitting with Billy Marr in a small interview room in the London Road police station. Grant had taken his tie off and was sitting back in his chair. Logan had her elbows on the table, her fingers together under her chin. She was looking at Marr, who was sitting opposite her. A cassette recorder was on the table, recording their conversation.

Logan spoke, 'Billy, I've been patient for as long as I can. But I'm beginning to get angry.'

Billy just looked at her without speaking.

Logan continued, 'You say you met this woman. She was young and blonde, and you strangled her on Calton Hill sometime in the early hours of this morning.'

'That's right,' said Billy. He was watching Logan carefully as if he wasn't quite sure what she was going to do.

'You see, my problem is this,' continued Logan. 'You won't tell me where you met this woman or what you talked about. You can't tell me who she was. You haven't told me how you managed to strangle her without her fighting back and leaving scratches on your face. And you've told me that you killed her on Calton Hill, but I know she wasn't killed there.'

'I killed her,' said Billy. 'I put my hands round her throat and strangled her.' He sat with his hands on his knees and looked at Logan.

Logan closed her eyes for a moment and then opened them again.

'Right,' she said, her teeth pressed tightly together in anger. 'I'm ending this interview, Billy. I'm keeping you here tonight and I'll want to talk to you again in the morning. And I'm warning you: I want the truth from you or you're going to be in serious trouble.'

Logan left the room with Grant close behind her.

Back in her office, Logan sat down heavily on her chair and threw her notebook on to the desk.

'Why does he do it?' she asked angrily, not expecting an answer.

Grant remained standing.

'If you want my opinion,' he said, 'I thought you were very patient.'

Logan looked up at him.

'Thanks,' she said.

Just then there was a knock at the door and Sergeant Graham came into the room.

'We managed to finish searching Calton Hill before it got dark,' he said.

'And?' asked Logan.

'Nothing, I'm afraid. There were a few old cigarette packets and things like that which we've sent to the scientists, but I'd be surprised if they find anything. And nobody there saw anything.' He put a piece of paper on Logan's desk. 'Names and addresses of the people who were there – in case you need them.' Logan gave the paper a quick look and then put it to one side. It was unlikely to be useful but you could never be sure.

'OK,' she said. 'Thanks for your help.'

Graham remained standing in the doorway.

'Is it right that you've been interviewing Billy Marr about this?' he asked.

Logan looked up.

'Yes. Why?' she asked.

'Well, I happened to see him last night.'

'Where was this?' asked Logan.

'Over on Lothian Road. There was a bit of trouble in an Indian restaurant. We were called. The trouble was nothing to do with him but he was in the restaurant.'

'What time was this?' asked Logan.

'About midnight. He was still there when we left at one.'

'Had he been there long, do you think?'

'Oh yes. One of the waiters mentioned that he'd come in early in the evening.'

Logan and Grant looked at each other.

'If he arrived early and was still there at one,' began Grant, 'then he can't be the killer.'

'So why does he say he is?' asked Logan. She looked at Graham and Grant but no-one spoke. She looked at her watch and took a deep breath.

'Right,' she said to Graham. 'Send Billy home but make sure he knows how angry I am. And if I catch him in here again telling us about something he hasn't done, tell him I'll . . .' Logan stopped to think about what she would do.

'I'll think of something,' said Graham.

Chapter 4 *Student life*

'Clare Rutherford. Aged twenty-five. She was a student at the university,' said Logan.

It was nine o'clock on Friday morning. Logan was sitting at her desk. Sergeant Grant had just come into the room.

'How do we know?' he asked.

'She shares a flat in Marchmont with a girl called Katie Jardine. Jardine reported her missing this morning.'

For many years the Marchmont area had been popular with students. A number of the university buildings were just a short walk away across an area of parkland called The Meadows.

'Twenty-five is quite old for a student,' said Grant.

'Research student,' explained Logan. 'She finished her degree course a couple of years ago and stayed on to do some research. She's in the Computer Science department. Well, she was.'

'What about Jardine?' asked Grant.

'Also a research student,' replied Logan. 'Apparently, Rutherford was going to a concert at the Usher Hall on Tuesday night. Jardine is from Glasgow and was staying at her parents' place in Glasgow that night. It was her father's birthday. She came back on Wednesday afternoon and when Rutherford hadn't appeared by late Thursday evening she called the police.'

'Are we sure it's Rutherford?' asked Grant.

'The body matches her description but we need to go

over and talk to Jardine now. Get someone to call the university or, perhaps better still, the Computer Science department and find out what they can: Rutherford's home address, a photograph if they have one, who directed her research, who her friends were. Tell them we think she's missing, but don't say we think she's dead. Not yet – not until we're absolutely certain it's her. I'll meet you in the car park in five minutes.'

Marchmont Road was a wide street with tall buildings on each side. The flat that Clare Rutherford and Katie Jardine shared was a light and airy second-floor apartment. The living room contained a sofa, a couple of armchairs and a TV, but as the flat was always rented out to students the furniture was neither expensive nor tasteful.

'When I got back on Wednesday afternoon and she wasn't here, I didn't think anything of it,' Katie Jardine was saying. She was short with rather wild dark hair. She wore blue jeans and a red sweater.

Jardine continued, 'But when she didn't come back on Wednesday night I got worried. I mean, we always told each other if we were going to be away for the night. She would at least have left a note. I'm sure she would.'

'Have you been in touch with any of her friends?' asked Logan.

'Yes,' said Jardine. 'Everyone I could think of. No-one saw her at the university on Wednesday or Thursday.'

'Boyfriends?' asked Grant.

'No.' Jardine shook her head and smiled at Grant. 'I mean, it's not as if guys aren't interested in her. She's very popular. But, well, she always says she doesn't want to get tied down in a relationship. Not yet anyway. She's from

New Zealand. Her grandparents were Scots – that's why she came here to university. But even though she's been in Scotland quite a while, she hasn't decided if she wants to stay.'

'Have you looked round the flat and in her room? Has anything been taken?' asked Logan.

'Not that I can see. All her things seem to be here.'

'Do you have a photo of her?' asked Logan.

'No,' said Jardine, 'I don't. But there are quite a few photos in her room. There might be one of her there.'

'Does she ever wear a pink T-shirt and a dark blue skirt?'

Jardine's hand went up to her mouth 'Yes, sometimes,' she said, almost in a whisper. And as she spoke, a tear started down her cheek. 'You've found her, haven't you?'

Logan put her hand on Jardine's arm. 'We're not sure about anything just yet,' she said gently. 'Is it OK if we have a look in her room?'

When Jardine nodded through her tears, Logan looked at Grant who left the room to look round the rest of the flat.

Half an hour later, Logan and Grant were sitting in Logan's car on Marchmont Road. Grant was holding a list of the names and addresses of Rutherford's friends that Katie Jardine had given him. Logan was looking at a photograph of Clare Rutherford that Grant had found in her room.

'Apparently, Rutherford's supervisor is a guy called Dr David Balfour,' said Logan. 'He directs a lot of the research in the Computer Science department.'

Logan reached up to get her seat belt and pull it down.

'He's got an office in King's Buildings out on West

20

Mains Road,' she continued. 'I suggest we go and see him. We're going to need someone to look at the body and tell us for certain that it's Clare Rutherford. We can't really ask Katie Jardine, can we?'

'No,' said Grant. 'It would break the poor girl's heart.'

'At least we think it would,' said Logan. Grant looked at her sharply. 'I'm sure you're right,' she said, 'but we still need to check that Katie Jardine was at her parents' house on Tuesday night.'

'True,' said Grant. One of the reasons that Logan was such a good detective was that she was careful. She checked everything, even the obvious.

Logan looked at the photograph again for a moment and said, 'Perhaps we should think about giving this photo to the newspapers and television, and asking for help from the public. We've very little information so far. We don't know where she met her killer, where she was killed or why.'

Grant looked at Logan. She was staring out of the car window, watching two boys kicking a football along the pavement. She had a good relationship with journalists – well, with one journalist really. It was a relationship that had been helpful in the past.

Logan smiled at Grant and then started the car.

'OK. Let's go and see Dr Balfour. While we're getting there, use your phone. Get someone to go to the Usher Hall to find out about the concert on Tuesday evening. See if they can find out where Rutherford was sitting and who was sitting near her. Maybe she met someone at the concert.'

Grant took his phone out of his pocket and Logan headed the car south along Marchmont Road.

Chapter 5　*Clare Rutherford's supervisor*

King's Buildings was a collection of ugly modern buildings set very close together in an area off West Mains Road. Dr David Balfour's office was in the James Clerk Maxwell Building. It was a grey, two-storey block with tall narrow windows, named after a famous nineteenth-century Scottish physicist. The building contained the university's Computer Science department, and a sign on the door read 'Edinburgh Regional Computing Centre'.

When Logan introduced herself and Sergeant Grant, Balfour came round from behind his desk to shake their hands. His actions were friendly, but he didn't smile and to Logan his eyes seemed to be grey, careful and rather cold. He was much older than her and had black, rather oily hair, combed very flat across his head. He was wearing an old, dark brown, patterned jacket and light brown trousers which looked as if they hadn't been cleaned for a long time.

'Please,' he waved a hand at two chairs in front of his desk, 'do sit down. How can I help?' He moved back and sat on the front edge of his desk.

Grant gave a small cough. Looking out of the corner of her eye, Logan saw that Grant had moved away from the chairs a little and wasn't going to sit down. Logan decided to remain standing too. She was as tall as David Balfour but if she sat he would be looking down at her. That was an advantage she did not want him to have.

'Thank you,' she said. 'I'll stand.'

Balfour said nothing. He looked at Grant and then back at Logan, and smiled. Not nervously, thought Logan, which was what most people did when the police walked in. It was more of an unpleasant smile.

'Dr Balfour, I'm afraid I've got some bad news for you,' said Logan.

'Oh,' replied Balfour, and the smile dropped from his face.

'I understand you direct the work of a research student called Clare Rutherford.' Logan paused as Balfour nodded agreement. 'Well,' Logan continued, 'we found a dead body on Calton Hill yesterday evening which we believe to be her.'

'Oh no!' Balfour's hand went up to his mouth. 'God! That's awful! Poor Clare!'

Logan watched him carefully. He was saying all the right words but his eyes seemed to be without feeling. Perhaps they were always like that. Then for a moment he looked as though he was going to cry. Logan and Grant looked at each other.

'How did she die? Was she murdered?' asked Balfour.

Logan looked back at Balfour.

'Yes, she was,' she said.

'Oh no! How awful!' said Balfour. He looked out of the window, lifted his head and bit his bottom lip.

'You directed her research,' said Logan, inviting him to tell her more.

'Well, yes, I did,' said Balfour, turning back to Logan. His eyes still seemed watchful. He went on: 'I have a number of students working on different research programmes. I check how they are getting on, make sure they know what they're supposed to be doing, make sure they explore all the right areas. And, of course, if they have any problems – research problems or personal problems – they can always come and talk to me.'

Logan wondered if students would want to take their personal problems to someone like Balfour. He did not seem an especially caring sort of person.

'And did she have any?' asked Logan. 'Did Clare Rutherford have any problems?'

'Not that I know of,' said Balfour, raising his eyebrows a little. 'She was very adult, very intelligent.'

'Popular?' asked Grant.

'Yes, she seemed to have a lot of friends.'

'A favourite one?' asked Grant.

'You mean a boyfriend?' asked Balfour, his mouth unsmiling, his eyes still empty of feeling. 'Not that I know of. No.'

'And how did you get on with her?' Logan asked.

'Very well,' said Balfour, his eyes narrowing a little. Undoubtedly he realised that he was now part of a murder investigation and that the police might be thinking that he was the murderer.

'She was an excellent student: hard-working, intelligent . . . yes, excellent.'

'And her research,' continued Logan, 'what was it about?'

'She was looking into wireless technology – ways of running computers and other sorts of hardware without having them physically joined together by wires.'

'I see.' Not knowing much about how computers worked, Logan didn't see at all. But she wasn't going to tell Balfour that. She would find out later.

'Did you meet her outside the university?' she asked, looking Balfour straight in the eye.

Balfour said nothing as he returned Logan's look.

'I don't think that's any of your business,' he finally answered quietly.

'This is a murder investigation,' said Logan equally quietly. 'Everything is my business. Did you meet her outside the university?'

'I took her out for dinner once or twice. But I do that with all my research students. I find it leads to a better relationship. But it's just dinner.' Balfour's eyes were hard now. 'Nothing else.'

'OK,' said Logan, easily. 'Now, I understand that Ms Rutherford's parents are in New Zealand.'

'Yes,' replied Balfour.

'The thing is,' she began, 'we need someone to look at the body and tell us for certain that it's her.' The colour started to leave David Balfour's face. 'Her parents are not in this country. We feel it would be very difficult to ask one of her friends. So we were wondering . . . I'm sorry to have to ask you to do this, but we really do need your help.'

Chapter 6   *Getting help*

Balfour had not wanted to see Clare Rutherford's dead body but Logan had pointed out that, as no relatives were available, and as he was her supervisor, he was the obvious person to ask. Finally they agreed a time for him to visit the London Road police station.

As they were walking down the steps in front of the James Clerk Maxwell Building, Grant turned to Logan.

'It's difficult to know what to make of him,' he said.

'How do you mean?' asked Logan.

'Well, he seemed quite friendly and helpful, except when you asked if he met Rutherford outside the university – though the fact that he wasn't so helpful then is perhaps understandable,' said Grant.

'But . . .' said Logan.

'But his eyes . . .' said Grant, leaving the sentence unfinished as they reached their car.

'Yes, his eyes,' said Logan, opening the door and getting in. She smiled at Grant and started the car.

'You find out about Balfour – his home life, his relationship with his students, that sort of thing,' she said, 'and I'll find out about his research.'

On their way back to the police station, the car phone rang. Logan turned on the speaker.

'Logan,' she said.

'Jenny, it's Helen Robertson,' said a voice from the speaker.

'Hi, Helen,' said Logan. 'What have you got for me?'

'Not much, I'm afraid, Jenny,' said Robertson. 'I've got no improvement on the time of death – about eighteen to twenty hours before she was found. And, as we thought, she was strangled. The only injuries are the bang on the back of the head and those that came from being strangled. So it definitely wasn't a sex attack.'

'What was she hit with?' asked Logan.

'Something wooden,' said Robertson. 'Possibly even just a piece of wood. You can see the square shape on her head where it hit her. And I've found a few tiny pieces of wood in her hair.'

'Her clothes?' asked Logan.

'Again, not much,' said Robertson. 'The clothes are very ordinary and certainly hers. There's nothing there to help find the killer except . . .'

'Yes?'

'There were some tiny bits of a sort of orange material sticking to the back of her T-shirt and her skirt.'

'What is it?' asked Logan.

'Well, from what I can tell, it's some sort of roof insulation material. You know, the stuff that people put in the roofs of their houses to stop the heat escaping in winter. I don't know how that might help you.'

Logan was quiet for a moment. Then she spoke, 'I guess it means that either she was kept in a shop or somewhere where they keep that sort of stuff; or else the murderer kept her in the roof of his house.'

She stopped speaking again for a moment while she thought. Then she said, 'Helen, if we find more of that material can you match it to what you found on Clare

Rutherford's body?'

'Well, yes,' she said. 'I can match it to similar material but this stuff is everywhere. However, if you find where she was kept, I'll almost certainly be able to show that she was there.'

'OK. That'll be useful. Thanks for phoning, Helen,' said Logan, and she turned off the phone.

It was midday when they arrived back at London Road. Grant went to find out more about David Balfour and Logan asked Sergeant Graham to organise a team of officers to interview Clare Rutherford's friends. Then she went up to her office to arrange some help. Sitting at her desk, Logan picked up the phone and tried a number she knew well.

'Tam MacDonald, Scottish Daily News.'

'Tam, my dear,' said Logan, 'it's Jenny.'

'Jenny,' said Tam, his voice warm and friendly. 'How are you?'

'Not great, actually,' said Logan. 'And I'm ringing to ask for some help.'

When Logan's friendship with Tam MacDonald, a journalist, had first come to the attention of Logan's senior officers, they had not liked the situation at all. They liked it even less when the friendship developed into a more serious relationship, but they had to admit that it had not yet been a problem. In fact, just over a year ago Tam had saved the police a lot of time by finding a criminal who had recently escaped from prison.

'What's the problem, Jenny?' asked Tam. 'You don't sound your usual self.'

Tam MacDonald usually joked with Logan about the

police asking journalists for help. However, he realised from Logan's voice that this was not a good time.

'I'm sure I don't,' replied Logan. 'I'm working on the Calton Hill murder. The main problem is information. We think we know who the girl is now but . . . ' Logan pushed her fingers back through her hair ' . . . it's just taking a long time to find out anything. I mean, she's been dead for thirty-six hours and her name is about the only useful piece of information we have.'

'That doesn't sound like the Jenny Logan I know,' said Tam. 'You're not usually so pessimistic. Tell me how I can help. And then I'll take you out tonight to cheer you up!'

*   *   *

The following day Clare Rutherford's picture was on the front page of the *Scottish Daily News*. Tam obviously had friends in television too as the photo appeared on a number of television news programmes. Anyone who had seen her on the Tuesday evening of her disappearance was asked to ring the London Road police station. Police were especially interested in anyone who had seen her at the Usher Hall or between the Usher Hall and Marchmont after the concert.

A team of officers spent the weekend answering calls. Although Grant and Logan investigated the more interesting ones they got no further in finding the murderer. Then on Sunday evening there was another disappearance.

Chapter 7 *Another student disappears*

'Frances Stewart,' said Sergeant Grant, reading information from his notebook. 'Called Fran by her friends. Aged twenty-five. University student. She has a room in a flat in the New Town – Drummond Place. The owner of the flat, a Mrs Dalwhinnie, rang in a few moments ago. Apparently, Fran went out to a party last night and she hasn't been back since. The party was at the home of one of her university teachers.'

'She might have just met some guy at the party,' said Logan, 'and gone back to his place.'

'I suggested that to Mrs Dalwhinnie,' said Grant, with a small smile, 'and she told me at some length what is wrong with the world today. Mrs Dalwhinnie has a loud voice and strong feelings about what is right and wrong.'

Logan smiled.

'Apparently,' Grant continued, 'Fran Stewart is the perfect young lady. Her parents are friends of Mrs Dalwhinnie, and she and Mrs Dalwhinnie go to church together every Sunday evening. That's why Mrs Dalwhinnie is sure that Fran is missing.' Grant spoke in a different voice, obviously trying to sound like Mrs Dalwhinnie: 'My Fran would never miss a Sunday evening without telling me.'

Logan smiled again and stood up.

'I think we'd better go and have a word with her.'

'I thought you might say that,' said Grant. 'She's expecting us.'

ESL
Library

Title: The University Murders

Author: Richard Macandrew

Name	Date In	Date Out

The New Town is the part of Edinburgh immediately north of Princes Street. It is still called the New Town, even though it is over two hundred years old. In some ways it is the most beautiful part of the city. It has wide streets and large squares with grand houses built around private parks. Mrs Dalwhinnie's flat was in one of these big houses.

Mrs Dalwhinnie was a big woman in her late fifties. She was wearing a grey dress with a grey, pink and blue scarf around her neck. She had attractive shoulder-length grey hair and wore half-moon glasses on the end of her rather large nose.

'I hope you are not intending to repeat any of the suggestions about Fran's behaviour that your sergeant mentioned over the phone,' said Mrs Dalwhinnie in her rather loud voice. 'Just because some young people have no idea how to behave properly, it doesn't mean that everyone is the same.'

'Indeed, Mrs Dalwhinnie,' said Logan. 'Sergeant Grant didn't mean to suggest that Ms Stewart would misbehave in any way. He was just exploring the possibility that there was another explanation for her disappearance.'

They were sitting in the living room in Mrs Dalwhinnie's flat in Drummond Place. The room was tasteful, with expensive, old-fashioned furniture, a piano in one corner and a large desk covered with papers in another corner.

'You told Sergeant Grant that Ms Stewart went to a party last night,' continued Logan.

'Yes,' said Mrs Dalwhinnie. 'She went with some of her friends from university. It was at the house of someone called Kenneth Henderson. He's her research supervisor.

She's not a student, you see – she's a research assistant – a very clever girl. Cleverer than her supervisor, if you ask me.'

Logan smiled. 'Where was the party?' she asked.

'Hope Terrace,' said Mrs Dalwhinnie, passing Logan a piece of paper. 'I've written the address down here for you.'

'Thank you,' said Logan, taking the paper. 'What's Ms Stewart researching?' she asked.

'Something to do with computers,' said Mrs Dalwhinnie, 'but I don't know too much about it.'

Logan and Grant looked at each other.

'Has she ever mentioned someone called David Balfour – Dr David Balfour?' asked Sergeant Grant.

Mrs Dalwhinnie thought for a moment.

'I don't think so,' she started slowly, 'but it's possible. We don't talk a lot about what she does because, as I say, I don't really understand it.'

Logan was quiet for a moment, thinking how strange it was that both Rutherford and Stewart were researching similar areas. Was it possible they were part of the same research programme?

'Did she know a girl called Clare Rutherford?' asked Grant.

'You mean the girl who was found on Calton Hill?'

'Yes,' said Grant, nodding.

'No,' said Mrs Dalwhinnie. 'We talked about that, of course. Fran knew who she was, but she didn't really know her'.

Grant had no more questions so he looked across at Logan.

'How did Ms Stewart go to the party?' asked Logan.

'She walked,' said Mrs Dalwhinnie.

'Even though Clare Rutherford had recently been murdered?'

Mrs Dalwhinnie seemed to sit up even straighter.

'Inspector, we cannot hide ourselves away. We cannot let a handful of criminals stop us from going about our daily lives. Fran walked everywhere in Edinburgh. It's one of the nice things about Edinburgh, don't you think? Although it's a city, it's small enough to walk just about everywhere.'

Logan agreed but she didn't say so. Instead she asked, 'And would she have walked home afterwards?'

'Of course.'

'Even if it was very late?' asked Logan.

'Yes,' said Mrs Dalwhinnie, looking away from Logan for the first time and out of the window. 'We always said that the streets of Edinburgh were safer than in other cities, Inspector. I'm just hoping we were right.' Her voice was not quite as strong as before.

*   *   *

Before they left, Logan asked for a photograph of Fran Stewart from Mrs Dalwhinnie. She also told her that they would make every effort to find the missing girl. On the pavement outside, Logan looked at her watch. It was already seven thirty.

'Let's go and talk to Kenneth Henderson,' she said. 'Then we might as well go home.'

Chapter 8   *The party at Hope Terrace*

Late on Sunday evening there wasn't much traffic on the way across town to Hope Terrace. A cold wind had started to blow in from the east and most people were spending the evening inside, in the warm. Although Hope Terrace was in the Marchmont area, it was very different from the street where Clare Rutherford had lived. These were houses for the rich, not for students.

'You can almost smell the money,' said Grant, breathing in through his nose as he pushed the doorbell.

Kenneth Henderson answered the door wearing a light blue denim shirt, and dark blue jeans with a light brown leather belt. He had bright blue eyes and dark brown hair that was quite long and combed back over his ears. He was in his early thirties and handsome, and he knew it.

He opened the door wide, looked first at Logan, then at Grant and then back at Logan.

'Kenneth Henderson?' asked Logan.

'Yes . . .' said Henderson. 'Inspector Logan and Sergeant Grant,' said Logan. 'We'd like to ask you a few questions.'

'Sure. Of course! Come in! Come in!' said Henderson.

Logan and Grant walked through a large square hall into a bright room with a light wooden floor. The furniture was all light wood too, with bright blue and yellow covers on the chairs and the sofa. Logan noticed a photograph lying on one of the tables. It was of Henderson with an attractive young woman. They had their arms round each other and were laughing. Henderson waved towards the chairs.

'Sit down,' he said, sitting down in an armchair himself and looking at Logan. 'What's this all about?'

'I understand you had a party last night,' said Logan.

'Yes,' said Henderson. 'Oh! I hope the neighbours haven't been complaining about the noise again.'

'Not that I know of,' said Logan. 'But a young girl who came to the party hasn't been home since. Fran Stewart.'

'Fran!' said Henderson. 'Yes, she was here. She left fairly early, as I remember – about one o'clock. I happened to notice what the time was when she came to say goodbye. But nobody else left until about four in the morning.'

Henderson seemed quite relaxed.

'Did you know Clare Rutherford?' asked Logan suddenly.

'Oh God!' Henderson sat forward. 'You don't think . . . the same thing has happened to Fran?'

'We're keeping an open mind,' said Logan, watching him carefully, 'but we're giving it our full attention.'

'Well, yes. I can understand that,' replied Henderson, getting comfortable in the armchair again.

'So,' repeated Logan, 'did you know Clare Rutherford?'

'Well, sure. I knew who she was. But we never had anything to do with each other, professionally . . . or privately,' said Henderson, giving Logan a big smile.

'Who else was at your party?' asked Logan.

'People from the university,' said Henderson. 'Students, teachers.'

'David Balfour?' asked Grant.

'Yes, David was here for a time.' Henderson smiled again. 'But he's not really a party animal. He probably left early.'

'What do you mean, probably?' asked Grant.

Henderson looked at Grant. Grant was sixty with thick black hair and a large black moustache. His clothes, as always, looked rather old: a blue jacket and grey trousers. He did not look much of a party animal either.

'Well, I don't check when my guests arrive and leave,' said Henderson. 'And some people just leave when they want to go home. They don't come and say goodbye. Anyway, sometimes I can be difficult to find.' Again he looked at Logan, raised his eyebrows and gave her a big smile. 'I sometimes end up in the bedroom.'

Logan looked at Henderson but did not smile. She was attractive and she knew it. But being attractive was not always a help to a police officer. Because she was good-looking, people did not always take her seriously. She did not like it when that happened.

'Your girlfriend?' She pointed at the photograph on the table.

'Ex-girlfriend,' said Henderson, stretching lazily and putting his hands behind his head. Still looking at Logan, he continued, 'The position of girlfriend is open at the moment. It's a great opportunity for the right woman.'

'A difficult position to fill, I would think,' she said rather sharply.

Grant looked across. Logan never got angry, even when questioning difficult people. But there was always a first time.

Henderson laughed and looked a little uncertain.

'Perhaps you'd be kind enough to give Sergeant Grant a list of everyone who was at your party,' said Logan. Then she stood up and started looking at the pictures and the books in the room, her lips pressed tightly together. In a little pile she found three photographs. She picked the photos up and looked at them: Henderson with three different young women. Obviously the position of girlfriend wasn't so difficult to fill – even though Henderson was, in her opinion, far too pleased with himself. Silently Logan warned herself to be careful. She must not allow any dislike of Henderson to affect the investigation.

She heard Henderson finish the list of names.

'I understand Ms Stewart was a research assistant. What was she like?' asked Logan, looking down at Henderson.

'Hard-working,' replied Henderson thoughtfully. 'Hard-working and not much fun. A bit too serious really.' Then he smiled at Logan. 'I mean, I invited her because I work with her, but I was surprised when she turned up. She really needs someone to show her how to have a good time.'

Logan said nothing. She just placed the photos carefully on the table by Henderson's chair.

'Thank you for your help,' she said. 'We'll be back if this becomes a murder investigation.'

Logan said nothing on the way back to the London Road police station. Neither did Grant. When they arrived there, it was almost nine o'clock.

As Logan turned off the car engine, she asked, 'What have you found out about David Balfour?'

'Only that he doesn't have a criminal record,' said Grant. 'But I've got a cousin who works in the university and I'm meeting him for a drink in half an hour.'

'Ask him about Henderson, too,' said Logan.

Chapter 9 *Another talk with David Balfour*

Monday morning started badly for Logan and soon got worse. Her kettle broke while she was making breakfast so she couldn't make a cup of tea. She then found she had set her video recorder wrongly and it had not recorded a programme that she wanted to watch. Things soon got much worse. When she arrived at the London Road police station, she was told that Frances Stewart had been found dead near Craigmillar Park Golf Course.

Driving out to the golf course, Grant told Logan what he had discovered about David Balfour and Henderson.

'Apparently there's a big question about Balfour's job at the moment. The university want to kick him out but they're having to be very careful.'

'Why's that?' asked Logan.

'Well, they want him out because he's not doing his job. He's OK at teaching and getting his students through their exams. But these days universities expect their staff to bring in money from research, especially the Computer Science staff. New technology makes good money.'

'And Balfour isn't bringing in good money?'

'No,' said Grant. 'He isn't bringing in any money.'

'So why are they having to be careful?' asked Logan.

'Well, his wife died last year after a long illness.'

'Ah!' said Logan, wondering if that explained his strange behaviour and dirty clothes.

'Everyone feels that his work has been poor because of

that,' explained Grant.

'I see,' said Logan. 'A difficult situation. And what about Henderson?'

'It seems he's the golden boy of the Computer Science department,' said Grant.

Logan made an impolite noise to show that she did not share this opinion.

'He's popular with students and staff, and he gets good results. But more importantly he manages to bring in a lot of money to the university.'

Grant said nothing for a moment then looked at Logan and smiled.

'But . . .' he said.

Logan smiled and waited for Grant to go on. She was pleased that there was a 'but' about Kenneth Henderson.

'. . . some people wonder if all the money that should go to the university from Henderson's work does actually go to the university.'

'You mean the big house?' suggested Logan.

'Exactly,' continued Grant. 'Not many people can afford a big house in Hope Terrace on a university salary and a research percentage.'

'What's a research percentage?' asked Logan.

'Well, if a researcher develops something that the university then sells, the university keeps a third of the money, the researcher's university department gets a third, and the final third goes to the researcher.'

'I see,' said Logan.

'Some people think Henderson is making too much money – that he must be keeping some back from the university. And . . .' Grant paused again to let Logan enjoy the fact that there was more to come, '. . . some people think he has not been completely honest about his research.'

'How do you mean?' asked Logan.

'Well, last year the university sold a computer program to an American company. There was some disagreement about who developed the program: Henderson or one of his students. In effect, people are saying he has stolen research from his students.'

Logan was quiet for a few minutes after Grant finished talking.

Finally she spoke, 'I need to find out more about what these girls were researching. It might be important. Also we need to know where Balfour was when Clare Rutherford was murdered. And what time he left Henderson's party and where he went. We didn't ask him before – but then we didn't know Frances Stewart was dead.'

'Right,' said Grant. 'By the way, we've checked and Katie Jardine was with her parents last Tuesday night.'

Logan and Grant arrived at the Craigmillar Park Golf Course shortly after Helen Robertson, the police doctor. The body was in a group of trees not far from the road. It was also not far from King's Buildings, thought Logan, and that might well be important.

Robertson was bent over the body as Logan and Grant reached the trees. She heard them arrive but did not look up. Eventually she completed her examination and stood up.

'I'm afraid it looks very similar to the last one,' she said. 'Off the record, I'd say you're looking for the same person who killed the girl at Calton Hill. I might be able to be certain later.'

The three of them stood looking out over Edinburgh for a moment. Arthur's Seat with its mountainous parkland was away to the left; Craigmillar Castle in the distance in front of them. Logan wondered who they were looking for. And why was this person killing? Was it to do with sex? Murder often was. Or was there another reason? Money, for example. Or could it be professional jealousy?

She took a deep breath and turned to look at the body. She recognised the face from the photo that Mrs Dalwhinnie had given her, even though the girl's tongue was sticking out and her face was blue round her mouth and lips. Like Clare Rutherford, Frances Stewart had been a pretty young woman, slim and with long, waist-length red hair. She lay now in a light green blouse and a long, dark green skirt, her beautiful hair falling over the green grass.

'Tell me about it,' said Logan.

'She was strangled too,' said Rutherford. 'But this time it looks as if the killer didn't use their hands. They might have used a scarf, or a belt or something like that. I'll tell you more when I've examined the body. Time of death, about midnight last night, give or take half an hour each way.'

'OK,' said Logan.

'Again there are no scratches on the body and no signs of any sexual activity that I can see. Though, of course, that doesn't mean that sex wasn't a reason behind the murder.'

'True,' said Logan. 'It's always a possibility.'

'Anyway,' said Robertson, 'I'll get you my report as soon as I can. Oh, and as before, her hands have been tied at some time.'

'Thanks, Helen.' Logan turned to Grant. 'Organise a search of the area. Then we'll go and see Dr Balfour again.'

Logan and Grant found David Balfour in his office on West Mains Road. He appeared to be wearing the same clothes as the last time they had met. As at their earlier meeting, Logan preferred to stand, not giving Balfour the opportunity to look down at her, also as at their last meeting she found his eyes odd.

'I'm afraid we've got some more questions for you, Dr Balfour,' she began.

'Never mind, Inspector,' said Balfour. This time he remained seated at his desk. 'I'm happy to help you if I can.'

Logan continued, 'First of all, we'd like to know where you were last Tuesday evening; and then we'd like to know where you were between ten and midnight on Wednesday evening.'

'Let me think,' said Balfour, pushing his hair back with his hand. 'On Tuesday evening I went to the Usher Hall. There was an Irish band playing that I wanted to see.'

Grant and Logan looked at each other.

'Who did you go with?' asked Logan.

'No-one,' replied Balfour. 'I went on my own.'

'What did you do after the concert?' asked Logan.

'I went home,' said Balfour. 'On my own.'

'Did you see Clare Rutherford at the concert?'

'No. I didn't know she was interested in Irish music,' said Balfour. Then suddenly he realised the importance of Logan's questions and his hand flew up to his mouth. 'Oh God! Was she at that concert before she disappeared?' he asked. 'How awful!'

'You're sure you didn't see her there?' asked Grant.

Balfour just shook his head and looked rather sadly at the desk in front of him.

'And what about between ten and midnight on Wednesday evening?' asked Logan.

Balfour thought for a moment. 'I was having a drink with some friends in Mathers.' Mathers was a bar in the West End of Edinburgh.

'Till when?' asked Logan.

'About eleven thirty,' said Balfour, still looking down at the desk.

'Names and addresses,' said Logan.

Balfour gave the names and addresses of three other university teachers, and Grant wrote them in his notebook.

'The other question,' said Logan, 'is what time did you leave the party on Saturday night?'

Balfour looked up quickly.

'What party?' he asked.

'Kenneth Henderson's party. You were there, weren't you?' asked Logan, but it wasn't a question.

'How do you know?'

Logan and Grant said nothing. They just looked at Balfour and waited.

Balfour looked from one to the other and realised he wasn't going to get an answer to his question.

'I left about twelve thirty,' said Balfour. 'I don't like parties much.'

'And afterwards?' asked Grant.

'Afterwards I went straight home.'

'Do you know someone called Fran Stewart – Frances Stewart?' asked Logan.

'I know the name because she's in the computer department, but I don't know her. She works for Kenneth. Why?'

'So you didn't speak to her at the party on Saturday night?' asked Logan.

'Not that I know of,' said Balfour.

Logan took the photograph of Fran Stewart out of her pocket and passed it to Balfour. Balfour took the photo and gave it a quick look.

'Yes, that's her,' he said. 'But I certainly didn't speak to her. To be honest I don't even remember her being there.'

Logan took the photo back. Balfour looked up.

'Why are you asking these questions?' he asked.

'Because Fran Stewart disappeared when she left that party and we found her body this morning,' said Logan. 'She's been murdered too.' Logan looked hard at Balfour. He shook his head slowly from side to side, a look of disbelief on his face.

Chapter 10 *Crossing the city*

Logan asked Grant to drive back to the London Road police station. She opened the car window and took some deep breaths even though it was a cool autumn day.

'There are some things that need checking,' she said to Grant. 'Find out where Balfour was sitting in the Usher Hall. I want to know if he could have seen Clare Rutherford while he was there. Find out who's interviewing the other guests at Henderson's party and make sure they ask if anyone saw Balfour and Fran Stewart in conversation at any time. And finally get hold of Billy Marr again.'

'Billy Marr?' asked Grant in surprise.

'Yes, I get the feeling he must have seen Clare Rutherford's body on Calton Hill,' said Logan. 'What I can't work out at the moment is why he thinks he killed her.'

Grant smiled. He had almost completely forgotten about Billy Marr, but it was no surprise to him that Logan hadn't. She often followed unusual lines of thought.

'And,' said Logan, as ideas continued to hurry into her mind, 'let's get a list of all the researchers in the Computer Science department and their supervisors. I don't know what we're looking for, but it might be worth a try.'

They pulled into the car park at the police station and got out of the car.

'And get some lunch,' said Logan. 'Then we'll go and see Henderson. I've got some more questions for "Golden Boy".'

Grant smiled. He went off to do what Logan had asked him to, while she went upstairs to her office.

At first she just stood and looked out of the window. There was a park on the other side of the road and children played in it at all times of the year – in sunshine, snow or even rain. She looked at the children playing there today and wondered what type of adults they would become: adults who worked, slept and played or adults who stole, fought and killed. She had been investigating murder cases for four years now. The job didn't seem to get any easier. She still found it difficult to accept the idea that one person could take another person's life. But they did.

She turned to look back into the room. On one wall was a large map of Edinburgh. She walked over to it and found the important places in the case: Calton Hill, the Craigmillar Park Golf Course. Her finger ran over the map.

Where had the killer met these girls? she wondered. Was it at the same place? Still thinking about this question, she picked up a pencil from her desk. Clare Rutherford was walking back from the Usher Hall to her flat in Marchmont. Logan drew a line from the Usher Hall to Marchmont Road. Fran Stewart was walking back to Drummond Place from the party in Hope Terrace. Logan drew a line from Drummond Place to Hope Terrace. Where did the lines cross? The Meadows. People did not walk in straight lines though, thought Logan, and she looked again at the map, working out the way that each girl might have chosen to walk home. Would they both have walked through The Meadows? Yes, they might. Was that where the killer met them? It was as likely as anywhere else, she thought.

Just then the phone rang. It was Helen Robertson.

'Exactly the same as on Calton Hill,' said Robertson. 'Everything the same: the bang on the head, the hands tied; she was strangled and there's that roof insulation material on the blouse and skirt.'

'OK. Thanks,' said Logan. She picked the phone up again immediately to call Tam MacDonald.

'Tam,' she said, 'I'm afraid I need your help again.'

'OK, Jenny,' he replied. 'And if there's a story for me at the end, that would be good too.'

Logan smiled to herself. Tam – ever the journalist. She told him a bit about the recent developments in the case and explained some of her thoughts to him.

'What I'd like you to do,' she continued, 'is to chat to some people up at the university and find out what's going on in the Computer Science department. Both the dead girls were doing research up there.'

'I'd be happy to, Jenny,' said Tam, 'but why don't you do it yourself? It is a murder inquiry after all. You can ask anybody anything.'

'True,' said Logan. 'But first of all, I don't understand much about computers and you do. And secondly, people are not so free with information when they're talking to the police. But if a journalist was writing about how the university is at the cutting edge of developments in computer science . . .'

'. . . they might tell me all sorts of things they wouldn't tell you,' finished Tam.

At three o'clock Logan checked that Henderson would be at home. On their way over to Hope Terrace Logan explained to Grant her thoughts about The Meadows.

'It's quite well lit, The Meadows,' said Grant. 'I mean, there aren't many dark corners where you can hit someone over the head, tie them up and take them away.'

'No,' said Logan. 'I don't think that's what happened. I think the killer must have picked the girls up there and taken them somewhere else. Either the killer is very good at persuading people to go with him or else the killer knew both the girls. And the girls weren't afraid of him.'

'Or her,' finished Grant.

'Right,' said Logan. 'Now, Fran Stewart went missing on a Saturday night. I think it's very unlikely that there would be any sort of regular pattern of movement through The Meadows on a Saturday night – you know, people who go through at the same time every Saturday. There's just people going out to pubs and clubs and restaurants, which they may or may not have done the week before.'

'But Rutherford went missing on a Tuesday night,' said Grant.

'Exactly,' said Logan. 'And it's Tuesday again tomorrow. Tuesdays are far less busy than Saturdays and there may be regular traffic – people going to and from work, regular Tuesday activities, that sort of thing. So tomorrow evening from, let's say, nine thirty to twelve thirty, I want to stop everyone in The Meadows and ask them if they saw anything unusual the week before.'

'OK,' said Grant as they pulled in outside Henderson's house. 'I'll get that organised for tomorrow evening.'

Chapter 11 *A slow investigation*

'Ah! the lovely Inspector Logan,' said Henderson, smiling at her as he opened his front door. He was wearing a pink shirt, light brown trousers with a brown leather belt and brown shoes. His teeth were a bright white.

Logan did not smile back.

'I said we'd be back if this became a murder investigation,' she said. 'It has.'

'Oh!' said Henderson. The smile disappeared from his face and he opened the door wider so that Logan and Grant could enter the house.

The living room looked exactly the same as the last time Logan and Grant had been there except for a copy of the *Scottish Daily News* on the table. Logan sat on the blue and yellow sofa. Henderson took an armchair near her. Grant stood by the door.

'Mr Henderson,' began Logan.

'Please call me Kenneth,' said Henderson.

Logan looked Henderson straight in the eye. Getting friendly with Henderson was the last thing on her mind. Keeping a professional distance seemed a much better idea.

'Mr Henderson,' she continued, 'what time did your party start?'

Henderson said nothing for a moment. He looked a little disappointed that Logan had refused to use his first name. Out of the corner of her eye, Logan could see Grant smiling to himself.

Henderson coughed. 'About eleven o'clock,' he said. 'A crowd of us went to the pub first. Then we came back here and a few more people arrived later.'

'When did Fran Stewart arrive?'

'She got to the pub at nine thirty. Something like that,' said Henderson. 'I really can't remember.'

'And Balfour?'

'I should think about eleven thirty. As I remember he didn't come along to the pub first. He usually just comes for a short time so that people see him. Then he leaves. Like I said before, he doesn't like parties much.'

'Did you see Balfour and Stewart talking to each other?'

'No, I don't think so,' replied Henderson, looking out of the window as he thought about his answer. 'Not that I remember, anyway.'

'OK,' said Logan. 'Who did speak to her, then?'

Henderson opened his arms wide.

'Come on, Inspector. I can't remember that. I understand this is a murder investigation and I'm very sorry about Fran, but I really can't remember who talked to who on Saturday night.'

Logan said nothing, waiting. Henderson stood up and walked over to the window. He turned back to look at her.

'Down at the pub everybody spoke to everybody. We were standing up and moving around all the time. When we came back here, I was too busy making sure everyone had a drink and something to eat and was looking happy.'

Henderson walked back to his armchair and sat down again.

'I spoke to Fran for about five minutes in the pub about her research and for about two minutes here when she came to say goodbye. Other than that I really didn't notice her. Like I said, she was a bit too serious.'

Logan sat back on the sofa and crossed one knee over the other. She brushed the leg of her trousers with one hand.

'I understand you make a lot of money for the university,' she said.

'Yes,' replied Henderson, looking rather pleased with himself.

'You must make quite a bit for yourself too,' said Logan, waving a hand to show that she was talking about the house.

'Oh no.' Henderson pointed at her. 'No, no. I know some people think I'm taking money that should really go to the university but that's not true. The house and everything here used to belong to my parents. They're both dead and the house is mine. I get a university salary and a third of any money that my research makes for the university. That's the arrangement with the university and I'm happy with that.'

He moved forward to the edge of the chair.

'And while we're talking about my work, you will also find people who say that I have stolen research from students and told people it was mine.'

'And that's not true either, I take it?' said Logan.

'Of course not.' Henderson was very certain. 'There are often "grey" areas about whose research is whose, especially when people are supervising researchers, but I always try to be extremely honest about it.'

Logan said nothing; she just looked at Henderson for a moment. It was impossible to know if he was telling the truth or not. Sometimes she knew when people were lying or telling the truth, but not always.

Then she asked, 'What exactly are you and your team researching at the moment?'

'Computer security. New ways of keeping information safe. Ways of stopping hackers – you know, people who get into computers to find out or steal information that they shouldn't have.'

'Mm,' said Logan, hoping that Tam got back to her quickly about the research going on at the university. 'What about David Balfour?' she continued. 'I understand he doesn't make as much money for the university as you do.'

Henderson took a deep breath.

'Poor David!' he said, shaking his head. 'He's a nice enough guy, but he's had a bad few years. What with his wife being ill and then dying. To be honest, the university is not very happy with him at the moment.'

Logan was silent for a moment, thinking about Henderson's answer. Then, changing the subject, she asked, 'Now, what about last Wednesday between ten and twelve in the evening? Where were you then?'

'Last Wednesday,' said Henderson, his eyes moving quickly from side to side as he thought about the question, 'I was here at home, preparing classes for the next day.' Suddenly, he realised why Logan had asked the question. 'Hey!' he said. 'Is that when Clare Rutherford died?' His face started to go red. 'You can't think I had anything to do with that.' He stood up angrily. 'That's crazy!'

'Anyone with you here on Wednesday night?' asked Logan, standing up herself.

'No,' replied Henderson.

Logan said nothing but just raised her eyebrows.

Henderson's shoulders went down. 'No. No-one was with me,' he said more quietly. 'But I had nothing to do with Clare Rutherford's death, I promise you.'

Back at London Road, Logan and Grant sat in her office drinking tea and thinking about the case. There was a knock at the door and Sergeant Graham came in. He was wearing jeans and a black T-shirt under the same brown leather jacket he had been wearing when he had met Logan on Calton Hill.

'We've found out where Balfour was sitting in the Usher Hall,' said Graham. He had a number of pieces of paper in his hand which he looked at from time to time as he was speaking. 'The ticket office keeps all its records on computer. He and Rutherford were in different parts of the hall and on different levels. She was at the top in the cheap seats and he was at ground floor-level near the back. It's possible they saw each other but we can't say for certain.'

Graham paused, waiting to see if Logan or Grant had any questions. They didn't.

'We've also talked to everyone who was at Kenneth Henderson's party,' he continued, 'and we've had no luck there. Quite a few people talked to Fran Stewart; quite a few people saw her talking to other people. Nobody saw her talking to David Balfour. Everyone said she was nice but serious. Nobody was seen trying to chat her up and nobody left the party with her. We're quite sure about that. Some of the other girls were in the hall when she left.'

'Things aren't getting any easier, are they?' Logan said.

'Worse, actually,' said Graham. 'We can't find Billy Marr.'

'What?' said Grant and Logan at the same time and sat forward in their chairs.

'Well, he's not at home,' said Graham, 'and he hasn't been home all day. We've also had a look in some of the places where he usually spends time but so far no luck.'

Lines appeared on Logan's forehead as she thought about this development. Eventually she shook her head as if clearing her brain and said, 'OK. Just keep looking for him. Give his description to all the police officers out on the streets tonight. Let them know that we're looking for him.'

'OK, madam,' said Graham. 'And, finally, we have the list of researchers.' He gave some papers to Logan and some to Grant. 'I made copies for both of you.'

'Good,' said Logan. 'Both of you have a look through these.' She looked at Grant and Graham. 'Take them away and go through them. If you find anything interesting, let me know immediately. If not, I'll see you tomorrow morning.'

Grant and Graham left the room. Logan put the pile of papers on her desk and turned to look out of the window. Perhaps they would find out something useful at The Meadows the following night; Logan certainly hoped so. It had been almost a week since Clare Rutherford had disappeared. Rutherford was now dead and so was Frances Stewart. The longer an investigation continued, the less chance there was of finding the murderer.

Chapter 12   *An evening on The Meadows*

The Bruntsfield Hotel, not far from The Meadows, is a large comfortable hotel in Bruntsfield Place, a kilometre or two south of Princes Street. The hotel bar, called the King's Bar, is on the lower ground floor and has an entrance down some steps from the small car park at the front of the hotel. At eight thirty on Tuesday evening Logan and Grant were sitting in the bar. They had spent the morning sorting through the mountain of paper that the case was producing. Most of this was interview reports. There were interviews with people who were at the Usher Hall, interviews with friends of Clare Rutherford and Frances Stewart, and interviews with the guests at Kenneth Henderson's party. The two police officers had spent the afternoon making arrangements for the evening's activity. They intended to stop everyone who passed through The Meadows that Tuesday and find out if they had been there the week before.

Grant was dressed in his usual grey trousers and blue jacket. Logan was wearing a dark grey jacket and trousers and a peach-coloured blouse. She wore small earrings of a Scottish design but no make-up. Logan didn't often wear make-up and never at work. In front of Grant was a large glass of orange juice. Logan was drinking tomato juice.

Having spent the whole day discussing the case, they had now moved on to talking about Grant's garden, Grant's nephews and nieces, and what he and Mrs Grant were going to do when he retired in three months' time. Grant was sixty years old and was stopping work at the end of the year.

Logan picked up her drink and finished it. She looked at her watch. 'OK,' she said. 'Let's go and see who can remember what they saw this time last week.'

*   *   *

There are a number of paths across The Meadows with trees along them, and a road, Melville Drive, between The Meadows and another green area of parkland called Bruntsfield Links. Police officers were stopping everyone, both in cars and on foot. They showed photos not just of Clare Rutherford, but also of Frances Stewart and asked people if they had seen either of them. They asked especially if people had seen Clare Rutherford some time after the concert the week before. Logan and Grant spent their time moving between the different groups of officers and keeping up to date with what was happening. As Logan drew near one of these groups, she heard a voice she recognised.

'I think you'll find that I don't need to answer these questions. I've already spoken to Inspector Logan at some length,' the voice was saying. It was Kenneth Henderson and he was wearing an expensive and very fashionable brown leather coat. He hadn't seen Logan arrive but turned as soon as he heard her voice.

'I think you'll find you do need to answer these questions, Mr Henderson,' she said. 'We have discussed Wednesday evening, as I remember, but not Tuesday evening. Where were you then?'

Henderson looked at Logan.

'Inspector, on Tuesday evenings I always play squash at the Lothian Squash Club on Coates Crescent.'

'Until what time?' asked Logan.

'It depends,' said Henderson.

'What time did you leave the club last week?'

Henderson thought for a moment.

'I stayed for a drink afterwards. I guess I left about ten thirty.'

'And you walked back this way, along Lothian Road, past the Usher Hall and up here across The Meadows?'

'Yes,' said Henderson. 'I always do.'

'Did you see Clare Rutherford as you were walking home last week?' As Logan asked the question, one of the police officers held forward a photograph of Clare Rutherford for Henderson to see. Henderson waved it away.

'I know what she looks like,' he said impatiently, and then corrected himself in a more gentle voice. 'Looked like.' He looked at Logan. 'No,' he said, 'I didn't see her.'

Logan looked at Henderson for a long time without speaking. He had been walking past the Usher Hall at about the time that Clare Rutherford had disappeared. He might have been at home on his own when she was killed – but he might not. Frances Stewart had disappeared after leaving his party. He had certainly had the opportunity but why would he have killed these two women? His love life seemed important to him. Had he asked both women out and they had refused him? It seemed unlikely. He had suggested that he was interested in Logan but hadn't been especially worried when she had not shown similar interest in him. Was it something to do with research at the university? Was that really likely? She could take him down to London Road for further questioning or she could make him sweat for a bit. She decided to make him sweat.

'Mr Henderson,' she said, 'you must admit it seems odd that Frances Stewart disappeared after your party and Clare Rutherford disappeared when you were both in approximately the same place. I'd like you to pop into London Road police station tomorrow sometime for a further chat about all this.'

Henderson took a deep breath.

'At a time that suits you,' said Logan. 'Say, four o'clock tomorrow afternoon.' And Logan turned and walked on to the next group of police officers.

*　　*　　*

The questioning continued through the evening, but they got no more information. At twelve thirty Logan walked over to a group of people standing on Melville Drive. She intended to thank the police officers for giving up their evening and to tell them to go home. However, as she reached the group, she saw a face she recognised.

'It's Katie Jardine, isn't it?' she asked.

'Oh! Inspector Logan. Hello,' said Jardine. Her hair was very wild today. 'How are you? Have you got any further with your investigation?'

'No, not yet, but we're still working on the case,' said Logan, and then looked at the girl who was with Katie Jardine. Jardine noticed Logan's look.

'This is Karen,' she said, 'Karen Ramsay; she's a friend of mine.' Karen Ramsay was easily 185cm tall, Logan thought, and she was big too. She looked older than Katie Jardine, probably in her late twenties. But, most noticeable of all, she had long blonde hair and an extraordinarily beautiful face.

Logan smiled at Ramsay, then looked back at Jardine and said, 'On your way home?'

'Yes,' she said. 'We've just been to the cinema. We stopped for a drink on the way back.' Jardine looked up at Ramsay as she spoke.

'Oh, I see,' said Logan, turning to Karen Ramsay. 'Are you a research student at the university too?'

'Yes. I work there part-time as well,' she added. Ramsay's voice was deep with a west coast accent. She looked Logan straight in the eye when she spoke to her. It was a look that made Logan feel a little uncomfortable, as if she shouldn't be asking Ramsay questions.

'Oh, yes?' said Logan, asking for more information without actually making it a direct question. The fact that she felt uncomfortable didn't stop her questions; it made her more interested in searching for information.

'Karen teaches at the university,' said Katie. Logan noticed Grant look more closely at Ramsay and begin to take more interest in the conversation.

'Just a few hours a week,' said Ramsay. 'I'm really doing research for a PhD – a doctorate.'

'You want to become a doctor?' asked Logan.

'Yes,' said Ramsay, 'a doctor of computer science.'

'Oh!' said Logan. 'You work in the computer department.'

'Yes,' said Ramsay.

'Right,' said Logan thoughtfully. 'So what's your research

all about?'

Ramsay looked down at Jardine and then back at Logan. She smiled.

'How much do you know about computers, Inspector?'

'Not much,' replied Logan. 'But I just wondered if your research was related in any way to what Clare Rutherford and Frances Stewart were doing.' The effect of Ramsay's stare was almost physical to Logan.

'Not really,' said Ramsay. 'I only knew a little about what they were doing. People don't talk too much about their research. Not until the research is finished anyway.'

'Professional competition?' asked Logan.

'Sort of,' said Ramsay, her eyes not leaving Logan's. 'It has been known for people to steal ideas. As a result, researchers don't usually talk too much about their work.'

'I imagine you knew Clare Rutherford, since she shared a flat with Ms Jardine.'

'Of course,' said Ramsay.

'You weren't by any chance in this part of town a week ago, were you?' asked Logan. She looked directly at Karen Ramsay as she spoke.

'Actually, yes,' said Ramsay. 'I usually work at the Bruntsfield Hotel – in the restaurant – on Tuesday evenings. I've got a week off, which is why I'm not there this evening. I was probably coming home about this time.'

Again Logan felt uncomfortable as Ramsay looked her in the eye.

'And did you see Clare as you were going home?' asked Logan.

'I'm afraid not,' said Ramsay.

Logan looked at her watch. 'OK, thanks for your help,' she said. 'You'd better get off home.'

'Thanks, and good luck with the investigation,' said Jardine as the two women set off towards Marchmont.

Logan watched them walk away and then turned to Grant.

'What did you think of Karen Ramsay?' she asked.

'She's tall,' said Grant, smiling.

'You got interested at one point in the conversation though,' said Logan seriously.

'Yes,' said Grant. 'That was when the university and the computer department were mentioned again. But I can't see how it could be important.'

'Nor can I,' said Logan, pushing her fingers back through her hair. 'And she was happy to tell us she was here last week. I just found her a little . . . well, I can't explain. Perhaps it's nothing to do with the case anyway.'

'Odd that she's working,' said Grant.

'Not really,' replied Logan. 'Students often have to work their way through university – even PhD students. A bit of teaching at the university, a bit of waitressing. It's quite normal really.'

Logan looked round The Meadows. There weren't many people still around at this time of night.

'Right,' she said. 'I think we're finished here. Not that we've got any further. Send everyone home and I'll see you in the morning.'

Chapter 13   *Computer technology*

Wednesday morning was bright and sunny, but the weather did not make Logan feel any better. To try and make herself feel a bit happier she wore a greeny-blue scarf Tam had given her last year. Eating her breakfast, Logan thought over everything that had happened during the last nine days. She didn't seem to be getting anywhere. She still didn't know where the girls had been killed or why. The three hours spent at The Meadows the evening before had seemed largely a waste of time. Kenneth Henderson was coming in for questioning, but even though she disliked him she did not feel that he was the person she was looking for. Karen Ramsay was a strange new addition to the case and Logan knew that she would have to find out more about the tall girl from the west coast. But could Ramsay have killed the two young women? Was it really likely? Logan shook her head, trying to clear her thoughts.

When she arrived at the police station, Tam MacDonald was waiting in her office. He stood up and kissed her lightly on the cheek. He could see from the look on her face that she was not in the best of moods.

'Don't ask,' she said, seeing his questioning look, but not wanting to talk about her problems. 'Just tell me what you've found out.'

She put her jacket over the back of her chair and sat behind her desk.

'They were very helpful up at the university when they

heard what I wanted to write about,' started Tam. 'They were especially interested when they heard there would be no dead women mentioned in the article.'

Logan smiled. Tam had a way of putting things which often made her smile.

'I spent a couple of hours with the Head of Computer Science yesterday afternoon. Essentially there are three main areas of research in the department at the moment. Computer languages is one area, the special languages that make a computer work; security is another area, how to stop people breaking into your computer; and wireless technology is the third area.'

'Tell me more about that,' said Logan. 'Balfour mentioned it. And it was Clare Rutherford's area of research.'

'Well, at the moment, if I want to, I can send information from my computer to yours. But the computers have to be joined by wires – either directly, or indirectly like over the internet. But with wireless technology I can put my computer on the table next to yours and, with the right software, they can talk to each other without being joined.'

'I see,' said Logan.

'Just don't ask me exactly how it works,' continued Tam. 'I know a bit about computers but not that much. Anyway,' he changed the subject, 'the university is apparently doing very well with its research into computer languages and into security. A lot of the research has been used in business and has made the university a lot of money.'

'And wireless technology?' inquired Logan.

'Well, that too has been a really important area of

research up until recently. However, the Head of Computer Science seemed to think that unless someone comes up with some new ideas or a new direction fairly soon they will think about cutting back in that area. At least for a while.'

'That's interesting,' said Logan, sitting back in her chair and wondering how David Balfour would feel about it. Did he need 'a new direction' badly enough to kill someone for it? After a moment she asked, 'Were Rutherford's research and Stewart's similar in any way at all?'

'I thought you might want to know that,' replied Tam. 'Since I'm not a police officer, it was a difficult question to ask without appearing very nosy. But after I'd spoken to the Head he got one of his researchers, a woman called Karen Ramsay, to give me a tour of the department.'

'Karen Ramsay?'

'Yes. Do you know her?'

'I met her yesterday too,' said Logan. 'Go on.'

'Well, working so closely with the Head, she knows what everyone is researching. So I just happened to mention the murders and I just happened to wonder if they were researching similar areas. Apparently not. They worked for different people, in different areas of research.'

'That's interesting. That's more or less what she told me,' said Logan. 'I wonder if it's true.' She stared out of the window at the park over the road and became lost in thought.

Tam sat quietly for a moment or two. Then he coughed.

'I'm off to work then,' he said.

Logan looked round suddenly. 'Oh sorry, Tam! I was just thinking about something.'

Tam looked at her carefully. 'Are you OK, Jenny?'

'Not really,' she said. 'The case is over a week old and we're getting nowhere. It's beginning to get me down a bit.'

Tam put his hand on Logan's shoulder. 'But you never know when your luck might change,' he said.

Logan smiled at him as he left the room.

A few minutes later, shortly after ten thirty, Logan phoned to check that Katie Jardine would be at home, then picked up her jacket and left the office. On her way out of the building she stopped at Sergeant Grant's desk.

'We need to find out more about Karen Ramsay, that woman we met last night,' she told him. 'See what you can find out by lunchtime. I'm going to talk to Katie Jardine. I'll be back this afternoon to speak to Henderson.'

Logan could have driven to Marchmont Road, but as she came out into the fresh air the sun was still shining. A good walk might clear her head and give her a fresh view of the case, she thought. The streets were busy with people shopping and enjoying the September sunshine. It was Edinburgh at its best.

Half an hour later Logan was walking past some of the university buildings. The shopping streets had been busy, but there were few people on the streets around the university. She heard a car slow beside her and a voice she recognised called out, 'If you're going up to Marchmont, I can easily give you a lift.'

Chapter 14   *Where is Inspector Logan?*

Kenneth Henderson arrived at London Road police station at exactly four o'clock. The front desk let Sergeant Grant know that he had arrived and Grant went to find Logan. Her office was empty and looked the same as it had that morning. Grant asked around in the offices near Logan's, but nobody had seen her since before lunch. Grant went back to Logan's office. It was unlike her to be late without letting him know. He picked up the phone in her office and tried her mobile number. It was switched off. That was strange. He searched through the papers on her desk and found Katie Jardine's phone number. The phone was answered after the third ring.

'Hello.'

'Ms Jardine?' asked Grant.

'Yes,' said Jardine.

'It's Sergeant Grant here, madam, Edinburgh Police.' Grant went on, 'I was wondering if Inspector Logan was still with you.'

'I'm sorry, Sergeant,' replied Jardine. 'What do you mean "still with me"? She never came. I thought she must have changed her mind.'

'Oh!' said Sergeant Grant. He was worried. 'She must have done. OK. Thanks anyway. I'm sorry to have bothered you.' And he put the phone down slowly. For a couple of minutes Grant stood there thinking. What was Logan doing? He had worked with her for four years now and he knew how she worked. She didn't go off on her own. If she was going somewhere, she told him where. Exactly as she had done that morning. He looked at his watch. It was five or six hours since she had left. Just then Sergeant Graham came into the office.

'Oh!' said Graham, when he saw Grant. 'I was looking for the inspector.'

'So was I,' said Grant, and explained the situation.

'Where else could she have gone?' asked Graham. 'What was she working on at the time?'

'She'd just asked me to find out everything I could about Karen Ramsay, Katie Jardine's friend we met the other night,' said Grant, looking through Logan's list of phone numbers as he had another idea.

Tam MacDonald answered his phone on the first ring. For the second time in as many minutes Grant explained the situation.

'She didn't say what she was going to do,' said Tam, 'but, yes, she was interested in Karen Ramsay. I'd found out that Ramsay was one of the few people in the Computer Science department who knew what all the researchers were doing. Jenny seemed to think that was interesting.'

'OK. Well, thanks anyway,' said Grant. 'I'm sure there's a natural explanation for all this. It's too early to start worrying yet.' But Grant's feelings did not match his words.

'I'm sure you're right,' said Tam. 'Listen, will you ask her to call me when she comes in. Just to let me know she's OK.'

'Sure.' Grant put the phone down slowly. Thinking fast, he turned to Graham: 'Kenneth Henderson, the guy who had the party, he's down at the front desk. The inspector wanted to interview him this afternoon. Let's ask him about Karen Ramsay.'

Five minutes later, Grant, Graham and Henderson were sitting in an interview room. A cassette recorder was on the desk recording their conversation.

'Mr Henderson,' Grant was saying, 'I understand that since she was the Head of Department's research assistant, Ms Ramsay would know something about each researcher's work.'

'That's right,' said Henderson.

'We know that both the murdered girls worked in the Computer Science department. And we know that they both knew Karen Ramsay. We're trying to decide how important this information is.'

Henderson sat and thought for a moment.

'I can't see how it could be,' he began, 'unless . . .'

'Yes?' Graham and Grant spoke together.

'Well, it's very unlikely,' said Henderson, 'but if she had seen how the research of the two women might be used together, perhaps something which no-one else had noticed, then, well . . .' Henderson opened his arms wide.

'What?' asked Graham impatiently.

'It would depend,' said Henderson. 'Possibly two pieces of research put together might be a great opportunity to make money. It might make even make her famous, I suppose.'

There was silence for a moment. Then Grant spoke, 'Mr Henderson, I'd like to know if there is any possible connection between the research these two women were doing. Would you be able to look into that?'

'Certainly,' said Henderson. 'I'll tell my boss to call you if he needs any further explanation.'

'No problem,' replied Grant.

*　　*　　*

Once Henderson had left, Grant spoke to Graham, 'Ring the university, find out where Ramsay is and meet me down in the car park. We need to talk to her.' Grant went back to his office to collect his jacket. As he walked from there down to the car park, he kept wondering what might have happened to Logan. He knew she was a very good police officer. She was intelligent. She was a good detective. She could look after herself. Grant didn't have any children, but if he had had, he would have liked a daughter like her. He knew as well as anyone that police work could be dangerous. He hoped that she was all right.

Grant and Graham reached the car park at the same time.

'Ramsay's not at the university,' said Graham. 'I've got her home address: Mayfield Gardens.' He started the engine and turned the car out onto London Road. Grant switched on the blue light; he did not want to waste time stuck in traffic.

Chapter 15 *Grant and Graham investigate*

Jenny Logan woke up in the dark. She had a terrible headache and her wrists hurt. She tried to move them but couldn't. They were tied together behind her. Was it day or night? And where was she? She turned her head and looked up. She could see bits of light above her. Little by little her eyes became used to the dark, and she realised she was in the roof space of a building. It was obviously an oldish building because of the light coming through the small holes in the roof. If she could see light, it must be day. She wondered if it was still Wednesday. Under her there were long pieces of wood going in one direction along the floor of the roof space. Between each of these was the kind of roof insulation material Helen Robertson had spoken about that kept heat in buildings. Logan could not see if it was orange or not. She had a feeling it probably was. This must be the place where the two murdered women had been kept. Was hers to be the third dead body found in one of Edinburgh's green areas?

Perhaps it hadn't been a good idea to accept a lift from someone who was part of a murder investigation, but it had seemed like a good opportunity to talk . . . Anyway, it was no use worrying about the past. She needed to think about the present. She needed to get out of here. Fast.

Logan tried to open her mouth but there was a piece of parcel tape stuck over it. She tried making a noise. It was possible but the sound was not very loud. Her feet were not tied so she started to move them round so she could get to her knees.

*   *   *

The police car pulled up outside a tall building in Mayfield Gardens. Grant and Graham got out quickly and entered the building through the front door. Just inside on the left was a row of postboxes, the name of the owner and the number of the flat on the front of each box.

'Here,' said Graham, pointing at the last in the row. 'Flat eight. Top floor.'

There was no lift, so they ran up the stairs. Graham took the lead; Grant, still healthy at sixty, was not far behind. There were two flats on each floor. Flats 7 and 8 were at the top: Flat 7 at the back of the building, Flat 8 at the front.

As they arrived at the door, Grant spoke, 'I'll ask the questions; you look out for anything unusual. If you get the chance, look around a bit.' Graham nodded. Grant knocked at the door.

A few moments later it opened.

'I'm Sergeant Grant, madam,' said Grant, holding up his ID card. 'We met the other night at The Meadows. And this is Sergeant Graham. I wonder if we could come in and ask you a few questions?'

'Of course.' Karen Ramsay opened the door wide to let the police officers into the flat.

The short hall led off to the left into a large comfortable living room. There were two closed doors on the right, and one open door straight ahead, leading into a small kitchen.

Ramsay closed the front door and followed them into the living room.

'Please sit down,' she said.

Grant and Graham sat, both of them looking round the room. There was a round dining table, piled high with books, and four chairs; a couple of armchairs and a sofa covered in a dark blue material; shelves full of books on computing; a desk with a computer on it; and another door that looked as if it led into a cupboard. A dark brown jacket hung over the back of one of the dining chairs, a greeny-blue scarf over the back of another.

'Ms Ramsay,' began Grant, 'perhaps you could tell us something about the research that Clare Rutherford and Frances Stewart were – '

The doorbell rang.

'Excuse me,' said Ramsay, going into the hall to answer the door.

Graham immediately stood up and started wandering around the room. He put his head round the door into the kitchen.

They heard voices at the front door and then Karen Ramsay saying, 'Well, the police are here,' and then, 'Sergeant Grant and I can't remember the other one's name,' and then, 'Well, come in and ask them if you want.'

The front door closed and Karen Ramsay came back into the room followed by Tam MacDonald.

'Sorry to interrupt you, Sergeant Grant,' said MacDonald, 'but I was hoping to ask Ms Ramsay a few questions. I just wanted to know how long – ' Suddenly he stopped as his eyes fell on the scarf over the back of one of the dining chairs.

'That's Jenny's,' he said.

Chapter 16   *Catching a murderer*

Inside the roof space, Jenny Logan had managed to move her legs round underneath her. Her eyes now used to the dark, she could just see a thin line of light around what seemed to be a doorway. Near it there was a small space where there was a proper floor. Logan stood up and began moving carefully across the space towards the floored area. Her legs felt shaky and it was difficult to balance with her hands behind her back but, keeping close to the wall, she moved slowly and quietly towards the doorway. There was the low sound of voices coming through. Logan held her breath and listened. There were both male and female voices, but she could not hear what was being said. Now that she was standing, Logan felt the strength returning to her legs. She felt there was a decision to make. She could stay quietly where she was and wait, or she could run against the door or kick it and see what happened. Usually Logan preferred to take action rather than wait for developments. She took three steps back, bending down where the roof came down towards the floor. She took a deep breath, then she pushed off hard, taking three short steps and throwing herself at the door in front of her.

In the dark, Logan had been unable to examine the door closely. Had she been able to see, she would have noticed that while the door was wooden, quite thick and well-made, the lock was small, cheap and easily breakable. Her shoulder hit the wood hard. The door flew open into

Karen Ramsay's living room at exactly the moment that Tam MacDonald noticed the greeny-blue scarf over the back of the chair. Logan fell into the room, hands behind her back, parcel tape over her mouth, dirt from the roof space over her clothes and hair.

Karen Ramsay had been prepared for trouble since Grant and Graham arrived at her flat. She was the first to act. Tam MacDonald stood between her and the freedom of her front door. Her elbow flew back hard into MacDonald's stomach. He made a strange cry as the air left his body and, his hands holding his stomach, he fell to his knees and then sideways to the floor. Ramsay raced for the door. Graham, who had been standing in the kitchen doorway, moved next. Jumping over MacDonald, he reached Ramsay as she was pulling the door open. There are times when the police try to do the minimum possible in order to hold or stop someone. Graham did not think that this was one of those situations; Ramsay was not only tall but strong. Graham took a handful of Ramsay's long blonde hair and pulled it back hard. Her head came back, her hands left the door, she screamed. She tried to turn, her hands reaching out, her fingernails like the feet of a wild eagle. But Graham was ready. His foot shot out, the kick landing on the side of Ramsay's knee. Her legs went from under her and she fell to the floor. Graham went down with her, still holding her hair, his other hand reaching for one of her arms. Ramsay started to fight back, but Graham caught an arm and, turning it quickly, he let go of her hair, put his knee in the centre of her back and pushed her wrist up between her shoulders. Ramsay cried out again.

'Don't move,' said Graham, breathing heavily and

continuing to hold Ramsay's wrist tightly so that she would not move.

Grant, realising that there was little he could immediately do to help from where he was sitting on the far side of the room, had bent down to help Logan. He carefully tore the parcel tape away from her mouth and started to untie her hands. Tam MacDonald had managed to get himself into a sitting position. His back was against the wall by the kitchen door, but he was still trying to catch his breath.

With her hands finally free, Logan stood up and moved quickly across the room to Tam.

'Are you OK, Tam?' she asked, kneeling down to put a hand on his shoulder and looking him in the eye.

Tam nodded rather than try to speak.

Logan stood up and brushed some of the dirt off her clothes. She looked at Sergeant Graham.

'Good work, Sergeant,' she said. 'Get her down to London Road with Sergeant Grant. I'll be along in a while.' Turning, she put out a hand to help Tam to his feet.

Chapter 17 *What Billy Marr really did*

The following morning, Logan and Grant were sitting in Logan's office on the second floor. Logan still had red marks around her wrists where she had been tied up. There was a knock and the door opened. It was Helen Robertson.

'Hi Jenny. I heard you were back at work already,' she said. 'How are you?'

'Not too bad, thanks,' said Logan.

'I was just passing,' went on Robertson, 'and I thought you'd like to know that the insulation material we found on the two murdered women is a match with the material found in the roof space at Karen Ramsay's flat.'

'Good,' said Logan. 'It all helps to make sure we have the right person and that she goes to prison.'

'Better still,' continued Robertson, 'they found some more material in the roof space at Ramsay's flat which is an exact match with Fran Stewart's skirt.'

'Excellent,' said Logan.

'So what was it all about?' asked Robertson. 'Why did she do it?'

Logan sat back in her chair holding a cup of coffee. 'It seems that it was all to do with research in the Computer Science department at the university,' she began. 'I don't understand it completely, but Kenneth Henderson explained the main ideas to me. Essentially, it's like this: two of the areas of research at the university are new wireless technology and computer security, and one of the main problems with wireless technology is security. For example, as I understand it, if I have the right equipment, I can park outside your office, log on to your computer, and then help myself to information without you knowing anything about it.'

'So why don't computer scientists just help each other find the answer to the problem?' asked Robertson.

'Well, apparently some researchers get very worried about other people stealing their ideas,' explained Logan. 'So they keep all their research very secret. However, there were a few people at the university who knew what all the researchers were doing –'

' – and Karen Ramsay was one of them,' finished Robertson.

'Exactly,' said Logan. 'She saw how two different pieces of research could work together to provide an answer – a brilliant idea that would not only get her a PhD but also make her rich. The problem was the two people who had actually done the research.'

'So she decided to kill them,' said Robertson.

'Right again,' said Logan. She looked across at Grant for him to finish the story for Helen Robertson.

'She knew both the women,' said Grant, 'so it was easy enough to offer them a lift. Presumably she followed them, waiting for a suitable opportunity. Late at night both of them would probably have been happy to accept the offer of a lift from someone they knew. After that it was easy.'

There was silence in the room as they thought about what Ramsay had done.

There was another knock at the door. Sergeant Graham looked into the room.

'Sorry to interrupt you,' he said, 'but do you still want to see Billy Marr? He's just been brought in downstairs.'

To Grant's surprise, Logan said, 'Actually, yes. Bring him up.'

'I'll leave,' said Robertson.

'No, no, Helen, wait. Come and sit down.' And Logan pointed to a chair beside her desk. Robertson sat down, looking a little confused. As a police doctor, she wasn't usually present at interviews.

A few minutes later Sergeant Graham showed Billy Marr into the room.

'Sit down, Billy,' said Logan. 'Now then, I want you to tell me exactly what happened two weeks ago when you found the woman's body on Calton Hill.'

Marr was about to open his mouth to speak, when Logan said, 'And no, don't tell me you killed her because we know who killed her and it wasn't you. Just tell me what you saw and did.'

'Well, I was up in the park there on Wednesday night – well, Thursday morning,' he began. 'Like I told you before.'

'What time?' asked Logan.

'I guess about two or three in the morning. I'd been out for a meal at an Indian restaurant. I'd had a few drinks and I was sitting against the wall close to the road and then I fell asleep. When I woke up, there was someone sitting further along the wall. I thought she was watching me. I sat there for a time and so did she. I told her to stop watching me, but she didn't.'

Marr's voice got louder.

'Was that a problem?' asked Logan.

'Sure it was,' said Marr. 'I didn't like her staring at me.'

'So what did you do?' asked Logan.

'I ran over towards her. I was really angry.'

'What did you do?' repeated Logan.

'I put my hands round her throat I was so angry,' said Marr. 'I didn't mean to kill her,' he continued, 'but I did. She made this horrible noise. I let go and jumped back but it was too late. She fell sideways and she was dead. Really, I didn't mean to kill her. It just happened like that.'

Logan looked at Helen Robertson.

'Billy,' said Robertson. She paused and waited until Marr looked up at her and she was sure she had his attention. 'She was dead when you found her. I'm absolutely certain of that.'

'But she made an awful dying noise when I put my hands round her throat,' said Marr.

Robertson thought for a moment. Then she spoke, 'Billy, dead bodies often make strange noises. They do strange things. Sometimes dead bodies even sit up. It can be very frightening if you don't know that it happens.'

Marr was quiet for a few moments as he thought about what Robertson had said.

'So you mean she could have made the noise even if she was dead?' he said eventually.

'Yes,' said Robertson.

Marr was quiet for a little longer. Then he looked at Logan. 'Thank you!' he said. 'I really thought I'd killed her. I really thought it was my fault. I didn't know why you wouldn't believe me.'

'OK. I understand, Billy,' said Logan. 'Now off you go. Sergeant Grant will see you out.'

Grant and Billy Marr left Logan's office. Helen Robertson went too, closing the door behind her. Logan stood up, stretched a little and looked out of her office window at the park over the road.

There was a knock at the door. Logan turned round as Tam's red hair and glasses appeared round the door.

'Hi, Jenny,' he said, coming in and letting the door close behind him.

'Tam.'

He took her in his arms and held her tight for a moment. Then he stood back, still holding her hands, and looked her up and down.

'How are you?' he asked.

'OK.' She nodded.

'I was worried,' he said.

Logan looked out of the window. 'So was I.'

'I don't suppose it's worth suggesting you do a different job.'

Logan looked at Tam and smiled.

'What do you think?' she asked.

'I think it's too important to you, you're too good at it and you're too lucky,' he said.

Logan took him in her arms and held him tight again.

'You're absolutely right!' she said. 'Especially that bit about being lucky.'